God Crea...

BIRDS

"In the beginning God created..." Genesis 1:1

God Created Birds

First printing: April 2023

Designed by Susan Windsor
Written by the ICR Communications team: Jayme Durant, Beth Mull, Michael Stamp, Lori Fausak, Bethany Trimble, and Renée Dusseau

ISBN: 978-1-957850-00-9

Please visit our website for other books and resources: ICR.org

Printed in the United States of America.

Cover image: Rainbow Lorikeet

God Created

BIRDS

ICR
INSTITUTE
FOR CREATION
RESEARCH

Dallas, TX
ICR.org

A WORD ABOUT BIRDS

Soaring high above trees, free as can be, birds can be colorful or downright wacky. But did you know there are about 10,000 species of them? That's a bunch of feathers in flight!

Birds come in all sorts of sizes. From the itty-bitty hummingbird to the ginormous stork, there are so many to explore.

When Jesus Christ created birds, He didn't just "wing" it—birds were carefully designed to live in habitats all over the world.

Cardinals

Peregrine Falcon

Swan

Emu

Fischer's Turaco

The Bible tells us that God made "every winged bird according to its kind," and He saw that it was good (Genesis 1:21). Even the smallest feathers are part of His awesome design.

Great Horned Owl

Male Mountain Bluebird

WHAT IS A BIRD?

Birds have feathers, but is that really what makes them...birds?

Well, all birds are warm-blooded and breathe air. They have wings and two legs, but none of the birds that exist today have teeth—that would make for some funny grins!

Birds lay eggs and often build nests. Many of them are talented singers. Some can sing two notes at once! Can you imagine what a choir of birds might sound like?

DID YOU KNOW?

Most birds have an egg tooth they use to break out of their shells, but it falls off after they hatch.

These baby birds just hatched and are waiting in the nest for their mother.

DID YOU KNOW?

Not all birds can fly. The penguin uses its wings for swimming, while the ostrich's wings aren't strong enough to lift its big body off the ground.

Emperor Penguin

Ostrich

RECORD-BREAKING BIRDS

Bee-lieve it or not, the world's smallest bird is the bee hummingbird of Cuba. It could make its nest inside a golf ball!

The extinct elephant bird of Madagascar is the opposite. This big bird stretched to nearly 10 feet tall. And the kori bustard is the heaviest flying bird. It can weigh over 40 pounds.

Some birds are expert athletes. The gentoo penguin is the quickest bird swimmer, with a pace of 22 miles per hour. And ostriches are the fastest runners, reaching speeds of over 40 miles per hour. If there were bird Olympics, they'd take home the gold.

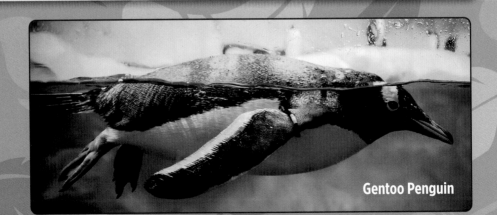

Gentoo Penguin

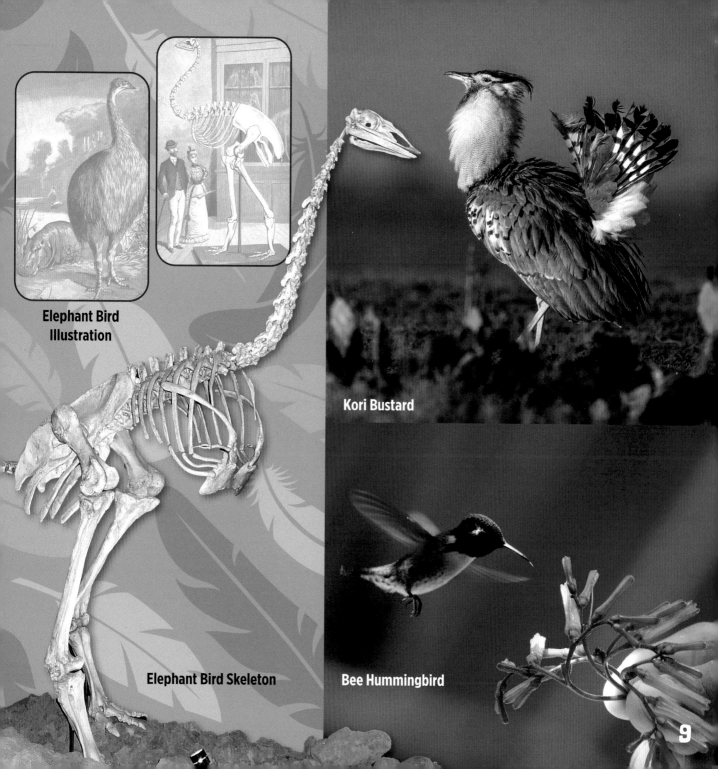

Elephant Bird
Illustration

Elephant Bird Skeleton

Kori Bustard

Bee Hummingbird

CHITTER-CHATTER, WHAT'S THE MATTER?

Birds are chatty creatures. They can make funny noises like hoots, gobbles, and quacks. Sometimes, they're really loud—especially in the morning! All the squeaks and squawks help them interact. Birds mostly talk with calls and songs.

Calls are short and simple. When a bird tweets, it has a specific purpose, like warning other birds of danger.

Songs are made up of musical-sounding notes. But they aren't just a performance—God has a purpose for them, too. These songs help birds defend their territory and attract mates.

Goose

European Robin

Mourning Dove

DID YOU KNOW?

Poets and artists have been inspired by the songs of birds since ancient times. Music composers like Vivaldi and Beethoven used instruments to depict birds in their work!

Antonio Vivaldi

Ludwig van Beethoven

Turkey

Northern Mockingbird

BEAKS, BIG AND SMALL

Bird beaks? So chic! The beak is an important part of the bird, and it's different for every species. Each size and shape illustrate Jesus Christ's expert handiwork. The design of a woodpecker's bill, for example, is exactly what it needs to hammer wood.

There are so many types, too. Wide beaks can break things like seeds or grain. Long, narrow beaks reach nectar in flowers. Large, sac-shaped beaks can catch and hold fish. Small beaks peck for insects and worms. God designed all these beaks with the tiniest details in mind.

Fiery-Throated Hummingbird

European Bee Eater

Black-Hooded Oriole

Great Spotted
Woodpecker

Great White Pelican

13

DIGESTION BY DESIGN

What would you need if you had to digest food without chewing it? A very strong stomach! Birds have tough tummies with two parts, the proventriculus and the gizzard. The first adds digestive juices, and the second grinds food into small pieces.

God created animals and plants to work together. Birds help some plants reproduce by spreading seeds or carrying pollen to flowers. Plants provide birds a source of food and habitation. It's a win-win!

Chickens

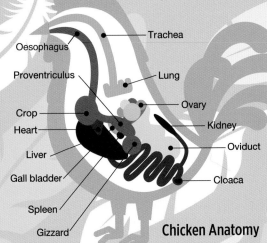

Oesophagus
Trachea
Proventriculus
Lung
Crop
Ovary
Heart
Kidney
Liver
Oviduct
Gall bladder
Cloaca
Spleen
Gizzard

Chicken Anatomy

The Gila woodpecker chisels its nest in a saguaro cactus. It eats the cactus' fruit and scatters its seed so the cactus can grow elsewhere.

DID YOU KNOW?

In birds of prey, indigestible bits like fur and bones are squashed by the gizzard into a ball called a pellet. The bird then coughs it up.

BIRDS OF A FEATHER

Birds wear lots of feathers! God made each type of feather for a specific purpose. Contour feathers cover most of the bird and protect it from sun, rain, and wind.

Long flight feathers on the tail and wing are designed to push against air and allow the bird to fly. And fluffy down feathers close to the bird's body keep it warm. And there are even more types than these!

Female Mallard Duck

White-Eyed Buzzard

God designed feathers with just the right materials and structures for flight.

DID YOU KNOW?

Contour feathers are hollow inside. It's a good thing, too—it'd be really hard to fly with all that added weight!

17

CRAZY COLORFUL BIRDS!

Are bluebirds actually blue? Well...not exactly. Very tiny structures in their feathers look blue when the light hits them, but they aren't blue on their own. It's the same with peacocks and hummingbirds—the colors change based on the angle you look at them.

Flamingos aren't naturally pink, either. They turn pink because they eat brine shrimp and algae with a red-orange pigment. Other birds are yellow, red, or orange because of the plants they consume.

Peacock

Flamingos

READY, SET, SOAR!

God gave special instructions to birds. In Genesis 1:22, He told them to "multiply on the earth." He gave them wings to travel.

There are many different types of wings. Passive soaring wings like those on eagles and storks are made for swift takeoffs.

Ocean birds like albatrosses and gulls have active soaring wings, which are long and narrow to glide over the sea.

High-speed wings help birds like the tern, duck, and falcon to fly— you guessed it—really, really fast!

Crows, blackbirds, and sparrows have elliptical wings that allow bursts of speed and tight turns. And hummingbirds have hovering wings that help them fly in one spot.

Sparrows

Stork

DID YOU KNOW?

Ravens like to do gymnastics! They can use their wings to somersault through the air.

Bald Eagle

Royal Tern

OPERATION: MIGRATION

Have you ever seen huge flocks of birds way up in the sky? They're probably following one of the avian superhighways— a stretch of four bird migration paths across North America.

These birds can cover thousands of miles to arrive at the same place every year. But they can't use a map, so how do they do it? Birds get direction clues from the sun and stars. God also gifted them with the ability to sense Earth's magnetic field. It's like their own internal GPS! Birds use these skills to navigate so they can reach the right spot at just the right time.

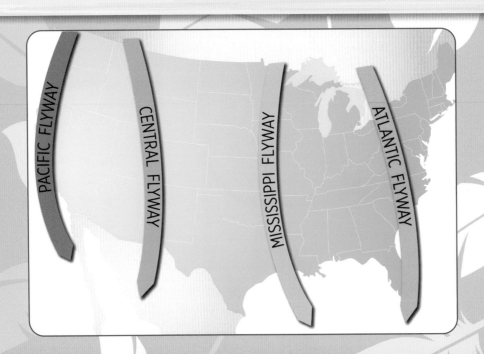

PACIFIC FLYWAY

CENTRAL FLYWAY

MISSISSIPPI FLYWAY

ATLANTIC FLYWAY

Canadian Geese

BIRDS IN HISTORY

Birds have kept humans company for thousands of years. Long ago, Egyptians adopted birds as pets. The British military sent hundreds of pigeons on intelligence missions during World War II. British author Charles Dickens kept a raven as a pet. Some birds, like the dove, can represent certain ideas or meanings—it's long been a symbol of peace.

Some ancient cultures like the Egyptians used the bird as an idol for their false gods. But God created birds. Psalm 50:11–12 says, "I know all the birds of the mountains...for the world is Mine, and all its fullness." He alone is worthy of our praise!

Pigeon

Dove

Raven

BIRD ORIGINS

The Lord Jesus made birds on the fifth day of creation. He created them with unique traits to live in their environments. In time, the many types of beautiful birds He created spread across the planet.

People who don't believe in God try to find other reasons to explain where birds came from. They teach a strange theory that over millions of years, dinosaurs became birds! But there's no way this theory could work. The fossils show that birds lived at the same time as dinosaurs.

Lovebirds

SIX DAYS OF CREATION

DAY 1

DAY 2

DAY 3

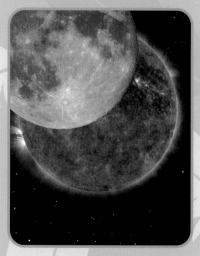

DAY 4

DAY 5

DAY 6

HALF BIRD? THAT'S ABSURD!

Look at this interesting fossil of an *Archaeopteryx*. Some scientists say it was part bird and part dinosaur.

But in reality, *Archaeopteryx* was fully a bird. It had wings, feathers, and the ability to fly.

God gave birds everything they need to thrive in the rainforest, the desert, Antarctica, and everywhere else on Earth. If God cares this much for birds, how much more does He care for you? The answer is He cares even more than you can imagine!

"Look at the birds of the air, for they neither sow nor reap nor gather into barns; yet your heavenly Father feeds them. Are you not of more value than they?" (Matthew 6:26)

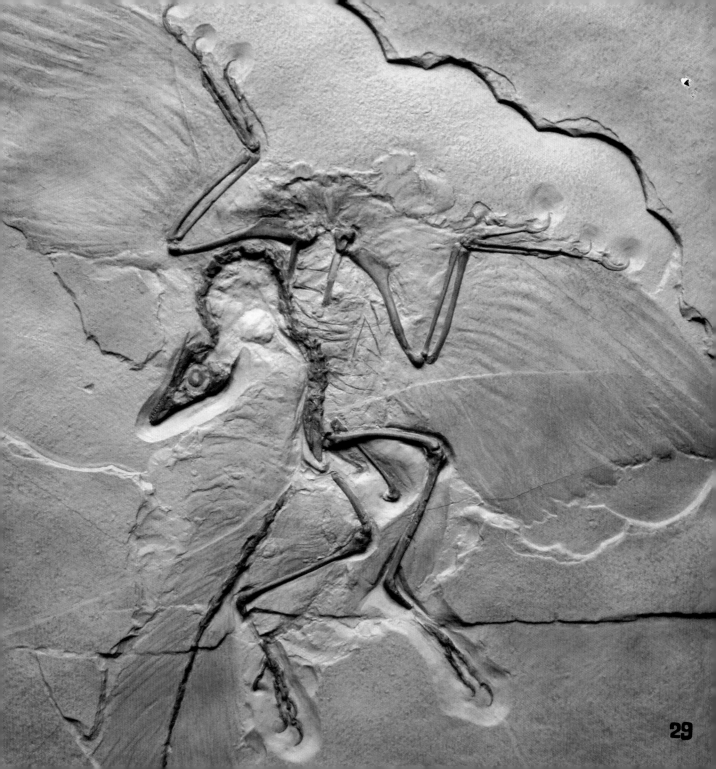

BIRD BLESSINGS

Noah Mosaic in Venice, Italy

In the Bible, a raven and a dove showed Noah when it was safe to leave the Ark. In Isaiah, the eagle symbolizes strength for God's people. Jesus pointed to the birds to show how much God cares for us.

God uses birds to illustrate amazing truths to us. The next time you hear birds singing outside your window, give thanks to God for His wonderful creation.

"But those who wait on the LORD shall renew their strength; they shall mount up with wings like eagles, they shall run and not be weary, they shall walk and not faint." (Isaiah 40:31)